playdate

with

GOD

WestBow Press books may be ordered through booksellers or by contacting:
WestBow Press
A Division of Thomas Nelson & Zondervan
1663 Liberty Drive
Bloomington, IN 47403
www.westbowpress.com
1 (866) 928-1240

Because of the dynamic nature of the Internet, any web addresses or links contained in this book may have changed since publication and may no longer be valid. The views expressed in this work are solely those of the author and do not necessarily reflect the views of the publisher, and the publisher hereby disclaims any responsibility for them.

Any people depicted in stock imagery provided by Thinkstock are models, and such images are being used for illustrative purposes only. Certain stock imagery © Thinkstock.

This book is a work of non-fiction. Unless otherwise noted, the author and the publisher make no explicit guarantees as to the accuracy of the information contained in this book and in some cases, names of people and places have been altered to protect their privacy. Scripture taken from the New King James Version. Copyright © 1979, 1980, 1982 by Thomas Nelson, Inc. Used by permission. All rights reserved.

Scripture taken from the King James Version of the Bible.

Scripture quotations taken from the Holy Bible, New Living Translation, Copyright © 1996, 2004. Used by permission of Tyndale House Publishers, Inc., Wheaton, Illinois 60189. All rights reserved.

Scripture taken from The Message. Copyright © 1993, 1994, 1995, 1996, 2000, 2001, 2002. Used by permission of NavPress Publishing Group.

ISBN: 978-1-5127-1820-1 (sc)
ISBN: 978-1-5127-1819-5 (e)

Library of Congress Control Number: 2015918042

Print information available on the last page.

WestBow Press rev. date: 11/11/2015

WESTBOW
PRESS®
A DIVISION OF THOMAS NELSON
& ZONDERVAN

playdate

with

GOD

A devotional for children and families

Kelly D. Holder, Ph.D.

Dedication

This book is dedicated to my children, Darby, Levi, and Kerith, who have taught me that you can hear God's voice even when you are playing.

A children's story that is only enjoyed by children is not a good children's story in the slightest. —C.S. Lewis

You shall love the LORD your God with all your heart, with all your soul, and with all your strength. And these words that I command you today shall be in your heart. You shall teach them diligently to your children, and shall talk of them when you sit in your house, when you walk by the way, when you lie down, and when you rise up. (Deut. 6:5–7 NKJV)

preface

More times than I can count, I have noticed the light in my children's eyes going out during worship time. I've tried many things to keep them engaged. We have colored and have even run and danced during the song time. I've purchased interactive books, only to find, I didn't have the necessary supplies on hand, such as glitter, construction paper, popsicle sticks, and so on.

One day, I played Hide-and-Seek with my children during our devotional time. That is when I got the idea for *Playdate with God*.

I wrote *Playdate with God* so you and your children would be able to experience God's Word while playing together. Play is integral to children's development. It's one way their minds process their experiences and learn about the world.

The book is divided into ten sections. Each section focuses on a different subject and has four chapters with games and devotionals that go with them. Many of the games will not be new to you. They are games that you may have played as a child. This book is unique in that each game is linked with a devotional, which is called "The Message," that connects the game with the Word of God. There are four devotionals in each section. This makes the book ideal for completing during the school year, doing one devotional each week for ten months.

Each section provides a memory verse. It also supplies a familiar tune you can sing the verse to. Singing will help you and your child remember the verse. Besides this, the only supplies you will need are your children and their receptive hearts.

As we teach our children about God, His love for us, and the awesome promises that are in His Word, we must engage our children in a way they can understand. My prayer is that your family's worship experience will improve as you use this book. I pray that you will begin to find more and more opportunities to play with your children as your family grows strong in the Lord.

Part 1

GOD LOVES US

The Memory Verse

The love of God has been poured out in our hearts. (Rom. 5:5 NKJV)

The Song

Sing the memory verse to the tune of "Mary Had a Little Lamb."

The / love / of / God / has / been / poured out,

been / poured / out,

been / poured / out.

The / love / of / God / has / been / poured out

i-/in / ou-/our / hearts.

Chapter 1

God Loves You More Than Anyone Else

The Game: Kiss, Hug, Chase

The parent will be *it* first. This game is just like tag, but, instead of tagging other people, you kiss or hug them. Make sure each child gets the opportunity to be *it*.

The Message

I love hugs and kisses, especially from my family. It tells me that you love me. My family loves me so much. I can't imagine anyone loving me more. Do you know that God loves you more than anyone else in the whole world? The Bible is full of stories about God's love. It tells us all of the wonderful things He has done and will do for us. I hope you will love Him too.

Additional Bible Reading

Psalm 36:5; Lamentations 3:22–23; 1 John 4:19

3

Chapter 2

God Will Look for You

The Game: Seek Sheep

The object of this game is to find the lost sheep. Choose one person to be the seeker. Blindfold the seeker or have him close his eyes. The rest of the family will be the sheep. The seeker tries to catch the sheep. The sheep try not to get caught by the seeker while bleating like sheep. Allow each child to try to find the lost sheep.

The Message

Jesus told a story that helps us know what God is like. The story is about a shepherd who loses one little sheep. The shepherd still has ninety-nine sheep left. What do you think the shepherd will do? This shepherd leaves his ninety-nine sheep. He looks all around until he finds the one lost sheep. He is so happy! He calls his friends and neighbors. He invites them to a party. If you ever got lost, God would look for you and find you. God wants to be with you because He loves you very much.

Additional Bible Reading

Luke 15:1–7

Chapter 3

God Watches Over You

The Game: Ring around the Rosie

Form a circle by joining hands. Walk in a clockwise direction with hands joined and sing, "Ring-a-round the rosie, a pocket full of posies, ashes, ashes, we all fall down." When you say the word "down," everyone stops walking and quickly sits down. The last one who sits down is out of the game and sits off to the side while the game continues. Repeat the game until there are only two people left. The first person who sits down first is the winner.

The Message

It's fun when we pretend to fall. While we enjoy pretending, no one likes to really fall and get hurt. My Bible says that God knows even when a tiny bird falls or gets hurt. If He watches over a tiny bird, don't you think He is watching over you? He knows everything about you. He even knows how many hairs you have on your head. Your mommy and daddy don't even know that! God knows you because He made you. He loves you very much.

Additional Bible Reading

Matthew 10:29–31; Luke 12:6-7

Chapter 4

God Will Find You

The Game: Hide and Seek

Choose one person to be the seeker. The seeker counts to ten or twenty, if she can, and everyone else hides. The seeker looks for each person. When she spots someone who is hiding, she calls out that person's name. When she has found everyone, the game is over. Play this game enough times so each child can be the seeker.

The Message

Have you ever lost your favorite toy? Have you ever lost something that costs a lot of money? Has mommy or daddy ever been upset because they could not find their keys? In the Bible, there is a story about a woman who had ten coins. One day, she lost one of those coins. She searched her whole house. She cleaned out her cabinets. She swept the floors. Finally, she found her coin. She was so happy. She invited all her friends and neighbors to a party. The Bible says that God has a big party when we decide to live for Him. Can you imagine God having a party in heaven to celebrate you? He loves you that much.

Additional Bible Reading

Luke 15:8–10

Part 2

GOD MADE THE WORLD

The Memory Verse

In the beginning God created the heavens and the earth. (Gen. 1:1 NKJV)

The Song

Sing the memory verse to the tune of "Ten Little Indians."

In / the / be-/gin-/ning / God / cre-/ate-/ed,

In / the / be-/gin-/ning / God/ cre-/ate-/ed,

In / the / be-/gin-/ning / God/ cre-/ate-/ed

The / hea-/vens / and / the / Earth.

Chapter 5

God Spoke Things into Life

The Game: Peekaboo

In this game, have the children cover their eyes with their hands. While your younger children's eyes are covered, ask questions, such as, "Where is mommy?" or "Where is daddy?" Tell them to uncover their eyes. Say, "Peekaboo. Here is mommy. Here is daddy." You can ask your older children about different objects in the room. You can say, "What color is the carpet?" or "How many chairs are around the table?" Parents should also take a turn at covering their own eyes and playing.

The Message

The Bible starts with this sentence, "In the beginning God created the heavens and the earth" (Gen. 1:1 NKJV). What was the earth like before God created things? Only God was there. Then God used His words to create everything on earth. It was the most amazing game of peekaboo ever! The sun, the plants, the animals, the people, and you were all created from God's wonderful imagination.

Additional Bible Reading

Genesis 1:1; 1 John 1:1–3

Chapter 6

God's Voice Is Powerful

The Game: Duck, Duck, Goose

For this game, ask your children to sit on the floor in a circle facing each other. Choose one person to be *it*. This person walks around the outside of the circle. As he walks, he taps each person's head and says, "duck." When he gets to the person he chooses to be *it* next, he says, "goose." He then must run from the goose. The goose must try to touch that person before he sits down in the goose's empty spot in the circle. If the goose is not able to do this, she becomes *it* for the next round and the game continues. If the goose is able to do this, the person who is *it* has to sit in the center of the circle. The goose now becomes *it* for the next round. The person in the middle can't leave until another player is tagged by the goose.

The Message

Do you think God created the animals by saying, "Duck, duck, goose"? That sounds silly, doesn't it? God did use His words to make the world. He said, "Let there be light," and there was light in the sky.

God's voice is powerful. Can you imagine your voice being that powerful? Can you imagine what it would be like if everyone turned into a duck or a goose while you were playing this game? God spoke and things became just what He said. God spoke and created a beautiful world for you and me.

Additional Bible Reading

Psalm 33:6; Hebrews 11:3

Chapter 7

God Made Ocean Life

The Game: Octopus Tag

In this game, the octopus tries to catch the fish. Your play area is the ocean. Choose one person to be the octopus. Everyone else is a fish. Have the fish line up along one side of the ocean. Have the octopus call out, "Come, fishies, come!" When she does this, all the fish must try to run to the other side of the ocean without getting caught. Once a fish is caught, he becomes seaweed and must freeze or sit where he is tagged. The seaweed can help the octopus catch the other fish by waving his arms and touching any fish that go by. When a fish is touched by seaweed, it becomes seaweed as well. The last fish that is caught becomes the next octopus.

The Message

On the fifth day of creation, God said, "Swarm, Ocean, with fish and all sea life!" (Gen. 1:20-23, The Message). Can you guess what happened? (Pause for guesses.) You are right! Fish, sharks, whales, sea stars, manta rays, sea horses, sea dragons, sea turtles, octopuses, and all sorts of other sea creatures filled the ocean. God spoke it, and it was done. It was beautiful. I enjoy looking at God's amazing creation. Don't you?

Additional Bible Reading

Genesis 1:20; Revelation 4:11

Chapter 8

God Has a Wonderful Imagination

The Game: Statues

In this game, you will pick up your child, gently swing him around, and set him on the ground. Tell your child to become a funny statue as you let go of him. Some examples would be making a funny face or holding his arm and legs in a strange position. Once someone becomes a statue, he should not move. After all family members become statues, the person who set them down picks out his favorite statues. He can pick as many favorite statues as he wishes. This is a great time to take pictures of your family having fun. Repeat the game as many times as you desire.

The Message

Did you like it when you were a statue? It is fun to create different poses. It feels good to create something new and to do something you haven't done before. Do you think God felt good as He made the world? Think of all the interesting things He made like bright stars, great big trees, tiny bugs, elephants that stomp, and alligators with their great big mouths. What other wonderful things did God make? (Pause for responses.) Just think that all of these things came from God's imagination. The best part is that He made them for you and I to enjoy.

Additional Bible Reading

Job 12:7–9; 2 Peter 3:5

Part 3

GOD MADE US

The Memory Verse

God created man in His *own* image. (Gen. 1:27 NKJV)

The Song

Sing the memory verse to the tune of "I'm a Little Teapot."

God / cre-/ate-/ed / man / in / His / own / image.

God / cre-/ate-/ed / man / in / His / own / image.

God / cre-/ate-/ed / man / in /His / own / image,

And / that / means / God / cre-/ated / you.

Chapter 9

God Carefully Created People

The Game: Jump to Your Feet

Have your children lay on the floor for this game. Then say, "If you are wearing pajamas, jump to your feet." If your child isn't wearing pajamas, she must stay on the floor. Keep calling out different reasons for your kids to jump to their feet. Make sure you use a mixture of things so they can jump up and lay down during the game. If your child does the wrong action, gently remind him what he is supposed to do.

The Message

God spoke the words, sun, stars, trees, flowers, fish, and birds, and they became what He said. God took a little more time when He made people. God didn't say, "Hey, Adam!" to create the first man. God sat down and created Adam out of clay from the ground. God took His time. He shaped all of Adam's parts. God made Adam to be just like Him. He made Adam in His image.

I think people are pretty special to God. That means you are pretty special to God, too.

Additional Bible Reading

Genesis 2:7; Ephesians 2:10

Chapter 10

God Breathed Life into People

The Game: Feather Breath Race

You need a very light object for this game, such as a feather or a small piece of paper. The object of the game is to see how far you can blow the feather or the piece of paper. The person who can blow the object the longest distance wins.

The Message

How strong is your breath? Can you blow very hard? My Bible says that God's breath is strong enough to make a person live. God created Adam, the first man, out of dirt. Then He blew His breath into Adam. Adam got up. He walked, sang, and played. Isn't that amazing? God created you, too!

Additional Bible Reading

Genesis 2:7; Job 33:4

Chapter 11

God's Power Gives People Life

The Game: Can You Make Me Walk?

The goal of this game is to see how hard it is to make someone walk. Stand up and have your children try to get you to take a step. At first, stand very still. If they are trying very hard, move your leg just a little bit. Another option is for you to lie down on the floor and let them lift your legs to see how heavy they are.

The Message

Have you ever made something out of play dough? What did you make? Did it get up and walk away? Of course not. That would be silly. God made Adam, the first man, out of clay from the ground. He breathed life into his body. Adam got up. He was alive! Adam was God's handmade creation. God made him walk, talk, run, and play. God's power gives people life. Guess what? God's power gives you life, too!

Additional Bible Reading

Genesis 1:26-28; Colossians 1:16

Chapter 12

we were made to Be Like God

The Game: Copycat

The object of this game is for your children to copy what you do. Pose and act in different ways. Make sure your children are engaged and are trying to be just like you. Allow other members of the family to be the leader.

The Message

It is fun to pretend to be like mommy or daddy. Sometimes you put on our clothes or try on our shoes. You may even do what we do. The Bible tells us that God created people in His image. That means God made us to be like Him. Since we can't see God, it's hard to copy Him and do what He does. But we have the Bible. The Bible tells us what God is like. That's where we can find out how to be like Him.

Additional Bible Reading

Genesis 1:26; 5:1–2; Ephesians 4:24

Part 4

GOD GAVE US RULES

The Memory Verse

If you love Me, keep My commandments. (John14:15 NKJV)

The Song

Sing the memory verse to the tune of "Twinkle, Twinkle, Little Star."

If / you / love / Me, / keep / My / commandments.

If / you / love / Me, / keep / My / commandments.

If / you / love / Me, / keep / My / commandments.

If / you / love / Me, / keep / My / commandments.

If / you / love / Me, / keep / My / commandments.

If / you / love / Me, / keep / My / commandments.

Chapter 13

we Can Follow God's Directions

The Game: Simon Says

Choose a family member to be Simon. Simon will give instructions to the family. Sometimes he will say, "Simon says," before the instructions and sometimes he will not. Participants should only act out the instructions if they hear, "Simon says," before the instructions. If a player makes a mistake, correct her and allow her to stay in the game. Each family member should have the opportunity to be Simon.

The Message

Simon Says is a fun game to play. You have to listen and follow Simon's instructions. Do you know the Bible is full of instructions? God gives us directions, rules, commands, and instructions so we will have a happy life. God created us and knows just what we need. Because He loves us, He gives us instructions to keep us safe.

Additional Bible Reading

Psalm 119:2; Proverbs 8:32; 1 John 5:3

Chapter 14

Stoplights Keep Us Safe

The Game: Red Light, Green Light

Choose one person to be *it*. Have family members line up, side by side. They should face the person who is *it*, and will be on the opposite side of the room. When the person who is *it* says, "Green light," the other family members will walk quickly toward that person. When the person who is *it* says, "Red light," the other family members will stop walking. This is repeated until all family members reach the person who is *it*.

The Message

Do your parents ever tell you to stop? Sometimes it's hard to stop when you are doing something fun. The word *stop* keeps you safe. Your parents can see things you can't see. They love you and want to keep you safe. It is always good to stop right when they tell you to. God loves you, too. In the Bible, He has given us many instructions. Even when we don't understand them, they are there to keep us safe and to help us live the best lives possible.

Additional Bible Reading

Leviticus 25:18; Luke 11:28

Chapter 15

All God's Instructions Are Good for Us

The Game: Mother May I

Choose a person to be the mother. Instruct family members to line up, side by side. Have them face the mother, who is on the opposite side of the room. The game starts with one person asking if she may take a certain number of steps. She also must ask for the type of step to take. The types of steps that can be used are baby steps, scissor steps, giant steps, jump steps, or karate steps. The mother will reply, "Yes, you may" or "No, you may not." The mother's answers depend solely on her whim. Each person asks the mother for permission until all family members reach her.

The Message

When I play Mother May I, I like it when the mother says, "Yes, you may." Yeses are great! The Bible is full of wonderful yeses. Yes, you may love and obey your parents. Yes, you may laugh and have a happy heart. Yes, you may do your best. The Bible also has some noes. It is hard when someone tells you, "No." But the noes are just as important as the yeses. They help keep us safe and allow us to live the best life possible.

Additional Bible Reading

Proverbs 3:5; 1 Corinthians 3:18-20

Chapter 16

God Uses Our Parents to Help Us

The Game: Follow the Leader

Choose someone to be the leader. The rest of the family lines up behind the leader. The leader walks around making funny movements and gestures. The other family members have to follow the leader and mimic the leader's actions. If someone does not do what the leader does, he should be gently corrected but allowed to remain in the game. Let several family members be the leader.

The Message

The Bible is our instruction book. It tells us how we should live. You should read it every day. It will help you live in the best way possible. But what if you are too young to read? God has given you parents. Until you are able to read the Bible for yourself, you can do what your parents tell you to do. God gave them to you. They will teach you how to live the way God wants you to. Trust your parents. Follow their examples as they lead you to God.

Additional Bible Reading

Deuteronomy 6:6–9; Ephesians 6:1

Part 5

GOD WANTS US TO OBEY

The Memory Verse

Children, obey your parents in all things, for this is well pleasing to the Lord. (Col. 3:2 NKJV)

The Song

Sing the memory verse to the tune of "Here We Go Loopty Loo."

Chil-/dren, / o-/bey / your / par-/ents

In / all-/all / things, / for

This / is / well / plea-/ee-/sing,

Plea-/ee-/sing / to-/oo / the / Lord.

Chapter 17

God Will Help You Obey

The Game: "The Hokey Pokey"

Get the whole family to sing "The Hokey Pokey." As you do, substitute different parts of the body for the word *hand* in this song. Here are the words to the song:

You put your right hand in, You put your right hand out,

You put your right hand in, And you shake it all about,

You do the hokey pokey, And you turn yourself around.

That's what it's all about!

The Message

It's fun to sing "The Hokey Pokey." The instructions in the song are easy to follow. Some things your parents tell you to do are easy like playing with your friends, eating your dessert, or sitting on your mom's or dad's lap when you feel sad. Other things are hard like picking up your toys or sharing with your brother. No matter how easy or hard it is to obey, God will help you. When He asks you to do something, He will help you do it. He loves you that much!

Additional Bible Reading

Proverbs 1:8-9; Isaiah 41:10; Colossians 1:10-11

Chapter 18

You Can Make God Happy

The Game: The Actions Game

To play this game, ask your children to follow the actions you demonstrate for them. Start with one action. If they are able to do that, add another action. You can add up to five actions at one time if your children are able to do them. You can use the following example:

Can you do this? (Touch your toes)

Can you do this? (Touch your toes, rub your belly)

Can you do this? (Touch your toes, rub your belly, jump up and down)

Can you do this? (Touch your toes, rub your belly, jump up and down, do a silly dance)

Can you do this? (Touch your toes, rub your belly, jump up and down, do a silly dance, spin around)

Use a variety of actions in this game. Allow all the children in your family to participate.

The Message

The word *pleasing* in our memory verse means to make someone happy. Do you know that God is happy when you obey your parents? You can make the God, who created the entire world, happy. But He even loves you when you don't follow directions. No matter what you do, you are special to God.

You are the most happy when you obey. When you follow your parents' directions, you are kept safe. I am so glad God gave me parents who protected me. Ask God to help you be obedient today.

Additional Bible Reading

Deuteronomy 5:16; Ephesians 6:1–3

Chapter 19

Obedience Isn't Just for Kids

The Game: Simon Clap

For this game, ask your child to clap in the same pattern as you do. Start with one clap. Then clap two times. You can do slow claps and fast claps. Continue playing by clapping three or four times in a variety of patterns.

The Message

Do you know that your parents have to obey too? They have to obey rules while they are driving their cars on the road. They have to obey the laws of their country. They even follow rules from God, which are in the Bible. Obedience isn't just for kids. When you learn to obey your parents, you are practicing to be an obedient adult.

Additional Bible Reading

Ecclesiastes 12:13; Romans 13:1; Hebrews 13:17

Chapter 20

Obedience Is a Treasure

The Game: Treasure Hunt

For this game, pick two or three things in the room that will be the treasure. After choosing the objects, describe each treasure (the color, shape, and type of object) and where it is located. Ask your children to find one of these treasures and to bring it to you (or stand next to it if it is too heavy). Repeat the game several times and allow all your children to participate.

The Message

Obedience is kind of like a secret treasure. It doesn't seem to be worth much, but it is pure gold. It is worth a lot. You may not always understand why you have to obey. And, that's OK. Trust that God gave you parents to protect you, to keep you safe, and to help you learn how to live the best life possible. God is their boss and asks you to obey them. When you make obedience a regular practice, it's like finding a secret treasure. It is treasure that can never be stolen!

Additional Bible Reading

Psalm 119:2; Proverbs 8:32; Ezekiel 36:27

Part 6

GOD SENT JESUS TO SAVE US

The Memory Verse

The Father sent the Son to be the Savior of the world. (1 John 4:14 KJV)

The Song

Sing the memory verse to the tune of "Brown Girl in the Rain."

The / Fa-/ther / sent / the / Son / to-/oo / be / the / Sa-/vior,

The / Fa-/ther / sent / the / Son / to-/oo / be / the / Sa-/vior,

The / Fa-/ther / sent / the / Son / to-/oo / be / the / Sa-/vior,

The / Sa-/a-/vior / of / the / world.

Chapter 21

Jesus Is Our Greatest Gift

The Game: Find the Paper Race

For this game, you need to draw a heart on a small piece of paper and then fold it small enough to be hidden inside a closed hand. Figure out where your finish line will be. The length to the finish line will determine how long your game will take. Have your children line up, standing side by side, and show them where the finish line is.

Secretly put the piece of paper, with the heart on it, in your hand. One at a time, ask each child to guess which hand has the paper and then open your hand and reveal whether he was right or wrong. Each time a child guesses the correct hand, tell him that he has won a gift and he may take one step forward. Continue the game until each child has crossed the finish line. When the game is over, unfold the paper and reveal the heart.

The Message

One of my favorite holidays is Christmas. It is the only holiday I celebrate for an entire month. I like to give gifts to my family and eat all the special Christmas foods. The best thing about Christmas is that it reminds me of the greatest gift anyone ever gave—Jesus. Jesus came to earth as a little baby. He grew up. Then He gave His life to save us from our mistakes. That means He will forgive us every time we mess up.

Additional Bible Reading

Isaiah 12:2; Luke 19:10; Romans 10:9

Chapter 22

Jesus Catches Us

The Game: Trust Me

To play this game, ask each child, one at a time, to stand with her back to you. Tell her you want her to fall backward and you will catch her. Have each child try this. Repeat the game as many times as you desire.

The Message

Have you ever fallen down while you were playing? When I was a kid I fell off my bike several times. It scared me. I didn't even want to learn how to ride my bike. But when my mom or my dad was with me, I wasn't so afraid to try. Why? Because someone was there to catch me if I fell.

Do you know that Jesus came to earth to *catch us*? He catches us before we fall into bad habits and sin. He saves us from our own mistakes. He forgives us. He gives us an example of how we should live.

Additional Bible Reading

Zephaniah 3:17; 1 Corinthians 10:13; 1 John 1:9

Chapter 23

Jesus Saved Us Before We Knew We Needed It

The Game: Blind Obstacle Course

For this game, choose one person to be the course runner and one person to be the helper. Blindfold the course runner. Once he is blindfolded, scatter items across the floor in front of him. Explain that he must go through the obstacle course. Even though he cannot see, he will have a helper who will guide him through the course so he won't hurt himself.

The helper can give him oral directions, can guide him with her hands, and, if the helper is a responsible child or adult, can pick up the runner to keep him safe.

The Message

Sometimes we know when something is dangerous—like crossing a busy street. At other times, we can't see the danger that is near us. Do you know that Jesus came to save us before we even knew we needed to be saved? You might not understand what this saving business is all about. Think about going through the obstacle course. You couldn't see the dangers that were there as you walked through it. In the same way, you may not see all the dangers in our world. Just like the helper in our game, God can see the dangers. He sent Jesus to help and to save us. This is the coolest thing I've heard all day!

Additional Bible Reading

Isaiah 42:16; John 3:16; Romans 5:6, 8

Chapter 24

Jesus Came to Take Our Place

The Game: Little Sally Saucer

In this game, choose one family member to be Sally. Ask the rest of the family to make a circle. Have Sally stand in the center of the circle. The people in the circle will walk around her and say this verse:

Little Sally Saucer sitting in the water,

Cry, Sally, cry, hide your weeping eyes.

Turn to the east, turn to the west,

Turn to the one you like the best.

Sally must close her eyes during the song. At the end of the song, have Sally point anywhere. The person she points at must take Sally's place. Allow each participant to have a turn to be Sally. Play this game even if there are only two of you. It will still be fun.

The Message

Poor, Sally. She is sitting in the water crying. Do you know why Sally is crying? Maybe she got in trouble for making a mistake.

I don't like to cry. I don't like to be in trouble. When you played the game, didn't it feel pretty good to get someone else to take your place? That's why Jesus, our Savior, came to earth. He took our place. He took our punishment for our sins. He didn't have to do it. He did it because He loves us so very much.

Additional Bible Reading

Isaiah 53:5; Hebrews 9:28; 1 Peter 2:24

Part 7

JESUS SHOWED US HOW TO LIVE

The Memory Verse

Therefore be imitators of God as dear children. (Eph. 5:1 NKJV)

The Song

Sing the memory verse to the tune of "He's Got the Whole World in His Hands."

Be-/ee / im-/i-/ta-/tors / of-/of / God

Be-/ee / im-/i-/ta-/tors / of-/of / God

Be-/ee / im-/i-/ta-/tors / of-/of / God

A-/as / de-/ear-/ear / chil-/il-/dren.

Chapter 25

We Should Copy Jesus

The Game: "Head, Shoulders, Knees, and Toes"

One parent should be the leader of this game. The goal of the game is to follow the leader, doing the actions and singing the song at the same pace. The leader should start the song slowly and then progressively get faster. The leader can then change the pace of the song from fast to slow or slow to fast. Allow other family members to take turns being the leader.

Head, shoulders, knees and toes, knees and toes

Head, shoulders, knees and toes, knees and toes

And eyes and ears and mouth and nose

Head, shoulders, knees and toes, knees and toes

The Message

An imitator is a person who copies what another person does. Have you ever copied your mom or dad? Do you copy your brother or sister? A teacher? A friend? Our Bibles tell us we should copy God. When Jesus came to earth, He showed us what God was like. We can be imitators of God by doing the things Jesus did. We can see all of the things Jesus did in our Bibles. Would you like to hear a story about Jesus? He is greatest person you can ever copy.

Additional Bible Reading

1 Peter 2:21; 1 John 2:6

Chapter 26

Get More Practice

The Game: I Went to the Store

For this game, all family members need to sit in a circle. The game begins when the first person says, "I went to the store to buy *vegetables* and I bought _____" (She chooses a vegetable to fill in the blank). The second person repeats what the first person said and adds his own vegetable. This pattern continues with each person adding his own vegetable. See how many vegetables you can name. If your children have difficulty with this task, you may simplify it by having them choose their vegetable first. Then you can say everything prior to their vegetable while pointing to each person who named them. The category can be changed to others, such as fruits or desserts.

The Message

Some people think it's easy to copy someone else. It isn't always easy. I like to watch cooking shows. I would love to copy what they do. When I try to make their yummy dinners and desserts, my cooking doesn't always turn out the way theirs do. However, the more I practice, the better I can cook. Copying God can be a like that. Maybe it's hard for you to be kind and loving or to forgive others. With God's help, the more we practice, the more we become like Him. Don't give up!

Additional Bible Reading

John 13:15; 1 John 3:2

Chapter 27

Focus on Jesus When You Are Confused

The Game: Telephone

In this game, your family needs to form a circle. Whisper a message in the first person's ear. That person whispers it to the next person, and so on, until the message gets to the last person. The last person will say what he heard out loud. Then you say the original message out loud. If there are only two people, whisper the message and then have the person tell you what he heard.

Here are some examples of messages you might want to use:

A beautiful beetle begged a butterfly for butter.

Sally soaks salty socks in sinks full of soda.

Tiny tangerines taste terrific on Tuesdays.

The Message

Those messages were very silly. Repeating silly things is fun. It is even more fun when the message is hard to repeat and gets sillier. When this happens in real life, it isn't very funny. Sometimes we copy the way other people act instead of God. The more we copy these people, the more we begin to do things that make our lives unhappy, unsafe, and unhealthy. I am glad that God gave us Jesus to copy. When we are confused about how to live for God, we can always remember Jesus's example and follow Him.

Additional Bible Reading

Romans 12:2; Hebrews 12:2

Chapter 28

Get to Know Jesus

The Game: Guess Who?

In this game, you will describe different family members. Start with very general descriptions and then become more and more specific, until your family can guess who you are describing. You may include any family members, whether they are present or not.

The Message

Was it easy or hard to guess who I was describing in this game? I think it might have been pretty easy for you. Why? Because you know these people really well. They are part of your family. I am sure you can pretend to be your mom or dad because you know us so well. If you want to copy God, you have to get to know Him and to spend time with Him. How do you do that? Sing your Bible verse songs. Read your Bible. Pray to God and tell Him about your day. Talk about Him with your family and friends. God loves you. He can't wait for you to get to know Him.

Additional Bible Reading

Proverbs 2:1–6; 1 John 2:3

Part 8

JESUS WANTS US TO PRAY

The Memory Verse

Never stop praying. (1 Thess. 5:17 NLT)

The Song

Sing the memory verse to the tune of "Frère Jacques (Are You Sleeping?)"

Ne-/ver / sto-/op

Ne-/ver / sto-/op

Pra-/ay-/ing.

Pra-/ay-/ing.

Ne-/ev-/ver-/er / sto-/op

Ne-/ev-/ver-/er / sto-/op

Pra-/ay-/ing.

Pra-/ay-/ing.

Chapter 29

We Can Pray Anytime

The Game: Don't Laugh Contest

The goal of this game is to *not* laugh. Choose one person who will be *it*. This person tries to make everyone laugh. Everyone else tries not to laugh. Allow each family member to be *it*.

The Message

It's easy to laugh. When something is funny, it's hard to hold a laugh inside you. God wants prayer to be just as easy for us as laughter is. We can pray with our families. We can pray before we eat. We can pray when we are alone in our rooms. We can pray on our knees. We can also pray while we are playing and having a good time. It's easy. Just say, "Dear Jesus, this is great! I'm having fun. Thank you!" It's that simple.

Additional Bible Reading

Colossians 4:2; Romans 12:12

Chapter 30

God Can Hear Our Prayers

The Game: Piggyback Rides

In this game, parents take turns giving piggyback rides. Give your child a ride throughout your home. Allow each child to have a turn.

The Message

Remember when we took our trip to _____ (fill in the blank). We walked a lot that day. Everyone was tired. Each of you wanted a piggyback ride. But I only have one back! Do you know that when you pray God hears you and answers all of your prayers? Unlike mommy or daddy, God can help all of us at the same time. We don't even have to stand in line.

Additional Bible Reading

Psalm 50:15; 91:15; Jeremiah 29:12

Chapter 31

Don't Stop Praying

The Game: Sardines

In this game, choose only one person to hide. The rest of the group counts slowly together to ten. Then everyone searches for the hidden person. When someone finds this hidden person, she quietly hides with him. As other players find those who are hiding, they join them. The game continues until everyone finds the hiding spot.

The Message

The Bible says we shouldn't give up when we pray. We should keep asking! This is the opposite of what your parents say, isn't it? Have you ever been told, "Don't ask for that again?" Jesus isn't like our parents. He wants us to keep asking Him. As we ask Him and get to know Him, He teaches us more and more about Himself. He answers our prayers in a way that helps us to live the best life possible.

Additional Bible Reading

Jeremiah 29:13; Luke 11:5–10; 18:1–8

Chapter 32

Jesus Can Hear Us Anytime

The Game: Three-Legged Walk

In this game, put your family members in pairs. Tie one person's leg to the other person's. Then have the pair walk through your home. Allow everyone to have a turn at being tied together.

The Message

Can you imagine anyone being closer to you than your family? What would it be like if you were tied to your parent, brother, or sister for the rest of your life? Do you think it would be nice to have them with you all the time? We have a friend who is closer than any brother, sister, or parent. It's Jesus. We can talk to Him anytime. It's even faster than a phone call or a text message.

Additional Bible Reading

Proverbs 18:24; Jeremiah 33:3; Hebrews 13:5

Part 9

JESUS FORGIVES US

The Memory Verse

If we confess our sins, He is faithful and just to forgive us *our* sins and to cleanse us from all unrighteousness. (1 John 1:9 NKJV)

The Song

Sing the memory verse to the tune of "This Old Man."

If /we / con-/fess / our / sins,

He / is / faith-/ful / an-/and / just

To / for-/give / us / our / sins,

An-/and / to-/oo / cleanse

Us / from / all / un-/righ-/teous-/ness.

Chapter 33

Jesus's Forgiveness Saves Us

The Game: Shoe Scramble

In this game, have all of the participants take off their shoes and place them in the center of the room. Mix up the shoes. Have the players stand against the wall. Let them know that when you say "Go," they must race to the pile of shoes, find their lost shoes, put their own shoes on, and race back to the wall.

The Message

Have you ever been lost? It's scary. It's good when someone finds you. Do you know that when we sin it is like being lost? When we sin, we do things that God did not create us to do. We aren't living the best life possible. Our sin gets us into scary problems. God has a solution for that. He forgives us. All we have to do is ask.

Additional Bible Reading

Psalm 103:10-14; Hebrews 8:12

Chapter 34

Jesus's Forgiveness Defrosts Us

The Game: Freeze Tag

Choose one person to be the tagger for this game. The tagger must try to touch other players. Once a person is tagged, he must freeze. He can only be unfrozen when he is touched by another player who is not the tagger.

The Message

Imagine what it would be like to really be frozen. You couldn't move. You couldn't talk. You couldn't even laugh. When I play Freeze Tag, I am happy when someone unfreezes me and I can run and play with my friends again. God's forgiveness unfreezes us. We don't have to be stuck in our sins and bad decisions. If we ask for forgiveness, God will forgive us.

Additional Bible Reading

2 Chronicles 7:14; Proverbs 28:13; 2 Peter 3:9

Chapter 35

Jesus's Forgiveness Never Runs Out

The Game: Windows and Doors

For this game, have your family form a circle. Have everyone join hands, stretching their arms out to form large spaces between each other. Choose one person to be *it*. This person runs around the circle, weaving in and out of the spaces made by the other players' arms. These are the windows and doors. Family members must try to catch the weaving person by putting their arms down to touch or to trap them. Once a person is caught, she gets to choose the next person who will be *it*. If there are only two people playing, the person who is *it* can run around the other player who has his arms straight out.

The Message

I remember when I was caught doing something wrong. I felt horrible. My parents were not happy with me. I felt awful for making a bad decision. You may think that adults are always trying to catch you doing something wrong. You might even think that God is trying to catch you doing something wrong. The truth is that God loves you very much. He is ready to forgive you when you are ready to ask. He wants to clean you and to help you live the best life possible. He has so much forgiveness and love to give to you. Don't stop asking Him for them. They will never run out.

Additional Bible Reading

Psalm 86:5; Ephesians 1:6-7

Chapter 36

Jesus's Forgiveness Is Always Available

The Game: Honey, Do You Love Me?

Have your family form a circle for this game. Choose one person to be *it*. That person goes in the middle of the circle. She must approach another family member and say, "Honey, do you love me?" That person must respond, "Honey, I love you, but I just can't smile." If he laughs or smiles, he is now *it*. The person who is *it* may not touch the other players but can make as many funny faces as he wants.

The Message

Do you know what temptation is? (Wait for responses.) Temptation is when you really, really want to do something. An example would be, wanting to laugh when something is funny. Not everything we really want to do is best for us. Sometimes we want to do things that can hurt us or our lives.

The good news is that God has a plan for when this happens. When we sin, mess up, or make the wrong choice, God forgives us. Never forget this.

Additional Bible Reading

John 3:16; Romans 5:8

Part 10

JESUS IS COMING BACK

The Memory Verse

Behold, He is coming with the clouds, and every eye will see Him. (Rev. 1:7 NKJV)

The Song

Sing the memory verse to the tune of "Itsy Bitsy Spider."

Be-/hold, / He / i-/is / com-/ing / wi-/ith / the-/e / clouds,

and / e-/very / eye / will / see-/ee-/ee / Him.

Be-/hold, / He / i-/is / com-/ing / wi-/ith / the-/e / clouds,

An-/and / e-/very / eye-/eye / will / see-/ee-/ee-/ee / Him.

Chapter 37

We Will Be with Jesus

The Game: Who Touched Me?

Choose one family member who will be *it* in this game. Have that person sit with her eyes closed or blindfolded. Ask her to turn her hands palm side up in front of her. Secretly choose another person to lightly touch her hand. Ask the person who is *it* to open her eyes and to guess who touched her.

If you are playing with only two family members, choose three objects. Touch the person who is *it* with one of the objects. She must guess what object you used.

The Message

Can you remember a time when we were apart? I remember missing you. When I came back, you were happy to see me. We talked and hugged and laughed together. We were happy to be together again.

Right now, the only way we can get to know Jesus is by reading the Bible and praying. The more we read our Bibles and pray, we get to know Jesus. Although we can't see Him, we can imagine what it would be like to be together. Won't it be exciting when we can see Jesus in person? I'm glad that He has promised to come back to earth and get us.

Additional Bible Reading

John 14:3; 1 Thessalonians 4:17

Chapter 38

Jesus's Return Will Be Worth the Wait

The Game: Father, Father, What Time Is It?

One person in the family is chosen to be the father. During game play, the father stands on one side of the room while the rest of the family stands on the other. Everyone chants, "Father, father, what time is it?" The father answers with a time he has picked, such as one o'clock. Everyone else jumps forward the same amount of times as he has named for his hour. For example, if he chose one o'clock, everyone would jump forward once. The father can also answer, "Time to come home." When he says this, everyone else runs toward the father and hugs him. Play this game as many times as you like. Let everyone have a turn to be the father.

The Message

I enjoy cookies that have just come out of the oven. Sometimes I get so excited about eating the cookies I can hardly wait for them to be done. Being patient is hard. The Bible tells us that no one knows the day or the hour when Jesus will return to earth. The Bible tells us that we have to be patient and wait. I do know that after Jesus returns we will be so happy. It will be worth any waiting we had to do.

Additional Bible Reading

Philippians 3:20; Titus 2:13

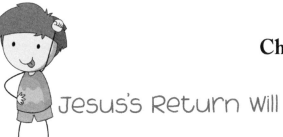

Chapter 39

Jesus's Return Will Be the Best Day Ever

The Game: Cocky Olly

This is a tag game. Before you play, designate an area that will be your base. The person who is *it* remains on base and counts to twenty while all the other participants hide. The player who is *it* looks for the others. When he sees someone hiding, he calls out "Cocky Olly. I see [name of person]." That person must then go to the base. Players can save those who are stuck on the base by touching them. The game ends when all players are on base.

To help make your devotional time more meaningful, make sure that at least one player is saved from the base during the game. If there are only two participants, use a timer to be *it*. Set the timer so that it is challenging for your child to hide in time. That way he might have to go to the base, and you will have the opportunity to save him.

The Message

When I play a game where someone is *it*, I do my best to get away from that person. You are the same way. When you call me for help, I run as fast as I can to keep you safe from *it*. Do you know that Jesus saves us too? One day, He will come and take us to be where He is. Then we will never have to worry about *it* again. There will be no more sadness, tears, hurt, or pain. It will be the best day ever!

Additional Bible Reading

1 Corinthians 2:9; Revelations 21:4

Chapter 40

When Jesus Returns, We Will Be Free

The Game: Freedom

For this game, you will need to choose an area that will serve as a prison. Choose another area to be home base. Choose one person to be the guard. Everyone else is on a team together. Pick one person from the team who will go to prison first. The team must figure out how to rescue the prisoner. A person rescues a prisoner when she makes it safely to the prison without being tagged. If she gets tagged, she becomes a prisoner, as well. The goal of the game is to save everyone from the prison.

If there are only two participants, allow a timer to be the guard. Initially, set the timer for a short amount of time. As the game continues, increase the amount of time you have to run so that you and your child are able to be free before the timer goes off.

The Message

Do you know what the word *free* means? When a person is free, she can live any way she wants without someone stopping her. I know that we will truly be free when Jesus comes back. Free to live with joy and gladness. We won't be stopped by pain, bad news, and worries. Most of all, we get to be with Jesus. I am looking forward to the day He comes back. I hope that you are too!

Additional Bible Reading

Isaiah 25:8; 51:11; Acts 1:10-11

About the Author

Kelly D. Darby Holder, PhD, is a clinical psychologist who has a passion for helping people learn how to live their best lives. Kelly has written devotionals, which have been published in *Help! I'm a Parent: Christian Parenting in the Real World* (Review and Herald Publishing, 2014). She serves her church as a children's ministry leader. Kelly's most prized task is her job as a mother of three lively young children. Kelly and her husband, Sheldon, live with their children in Harrisburg, Pennsylvania.

Additional resources for this devotional can be found on the web at:

www.playdatewithGod.com